Colors in My World

Green in My World

By Brienna Rossiter

level
1
little blue
readers

www.littlebluehousebooks.com

Little Blue House is distributed by North Star Editions:
sales@northstareditions.com | 888-417-0195

Produced for Little Blue House by Red Line Editorial.

Photographs ©: Shutterstock Images, cover, 4, 7, 8–9, 11, 12–13, 14–15, 16 (top left), 16 (top right), 16 (bottom left), 16 (bottom right)

Library of Congress Control Number: 2020900798

ISBN
978-1-64619-158-1 (hardcover)
978-1-64619-192-5 (paperback)
978-1-64619-260-1 (ebook pdf)
978-1-64619-226-7 (hosted ebook)

Printed in the United States of America
Mankato, MN
082020

About the Author

Brienna Rossiter enjoys playing music, reading books, and drinking tea. She lives in Minnesota.

Table of Contents

I See Green

I see trees.

The trees are green.

I see a light.

The light is green.

light

I see grass.

The grass is green.

I see a bench.

The bench is green.

I see a swing.

The swing is green.

I see a house.

The house is green.

Glossary

bench

house

grass

swing

Index

Colors in My World

From blue skies to green plants, colors are all around us every day. This fun series helps young readers spot the different colors in the places they live.

Books in this series

Blue in My World
Green in My World
Orange in My World

Purple in My World
Red in My World
Yellow in My World

little blue house

With simple text, vibrant photos, and high-interest topics, Little Blue Readers are an ideal way for young learners to take their first steps toward literacy.

ISBN: 978-1-64619-192-5

9 781646 191925

GRL: B

Colors in My World

Red in My World

By Brienna Rossiter

level
1
little blue
readers